*The Great Glen, as seen from the shore of Loch Oich near Invergarry, Highland*

**1**

New Year with
Winnie & George

**2**

New Year
At Greenbank
With George & Winnie
Drove home in the Afternoon
Snowing heavy

Pat Ingles
Phoned
~~Phoned~~
Pat
Honders
Phoned

**3**

~~Winnie & George~~
~~Drove~~ home in the Afternoon
~~Graham Phone~~
~~Snowing Heavy~~ No one Phoned
on My own all day

**4**

~~Phone Graham Phone~~

**5**

**6**

**7**

*Notes*

January

8

9

10

11

12

13

14

Notes

15

16

17

18

19

20

21

*Notes*

*The Forth Road Bridge, linking South Queensferry, Edinburgh, with North Queensferry, Fife*

22

23

24

25

26

27

28

*Notes*

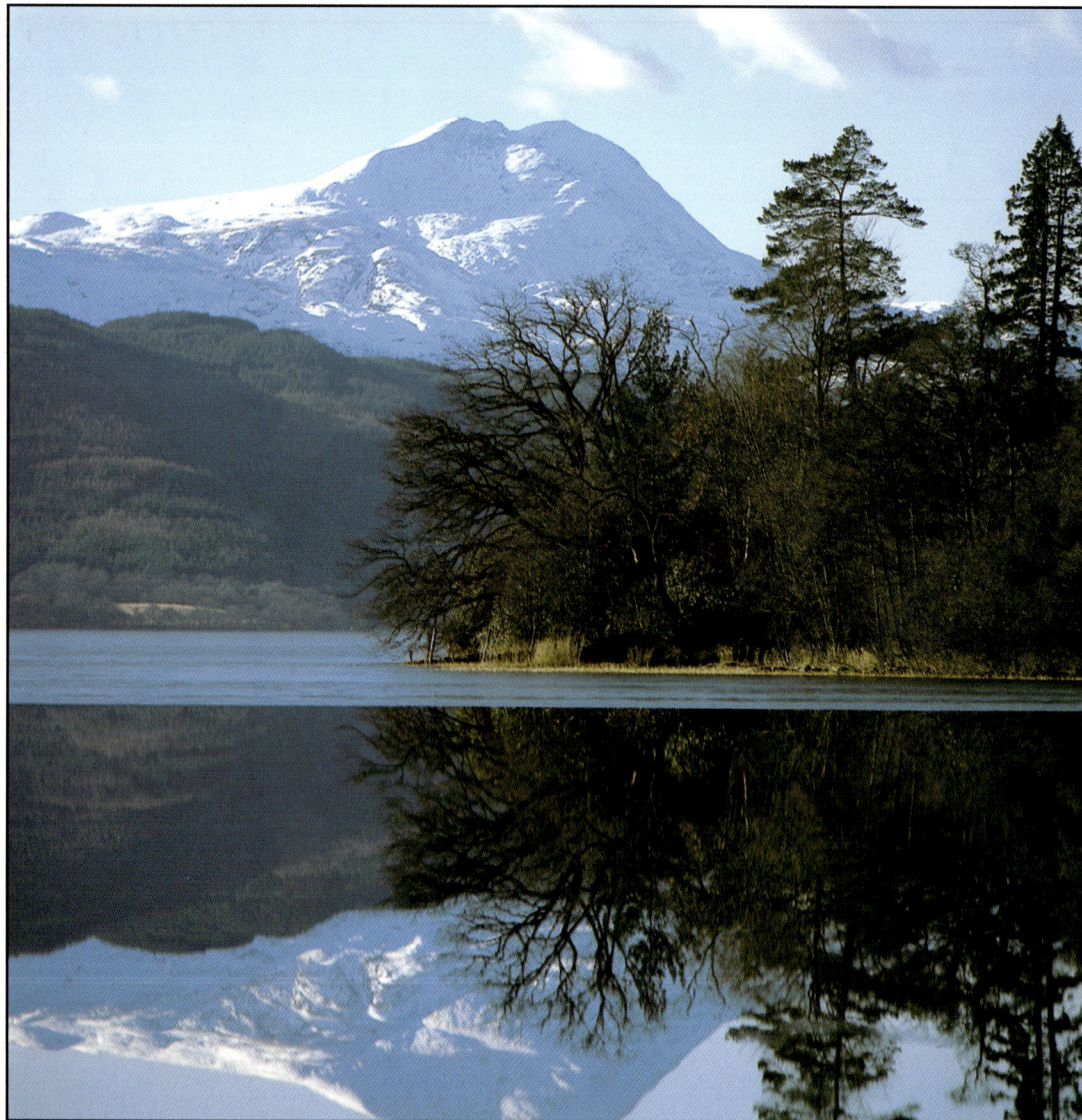

29

30

31

1

2

3

4

*Notes*

*Stirling, looking towards the Wallace Monument*

# February

5

6

7

8

9

10

11

Notes

*February*

12

16

13

17

14

18

15

*Notes*

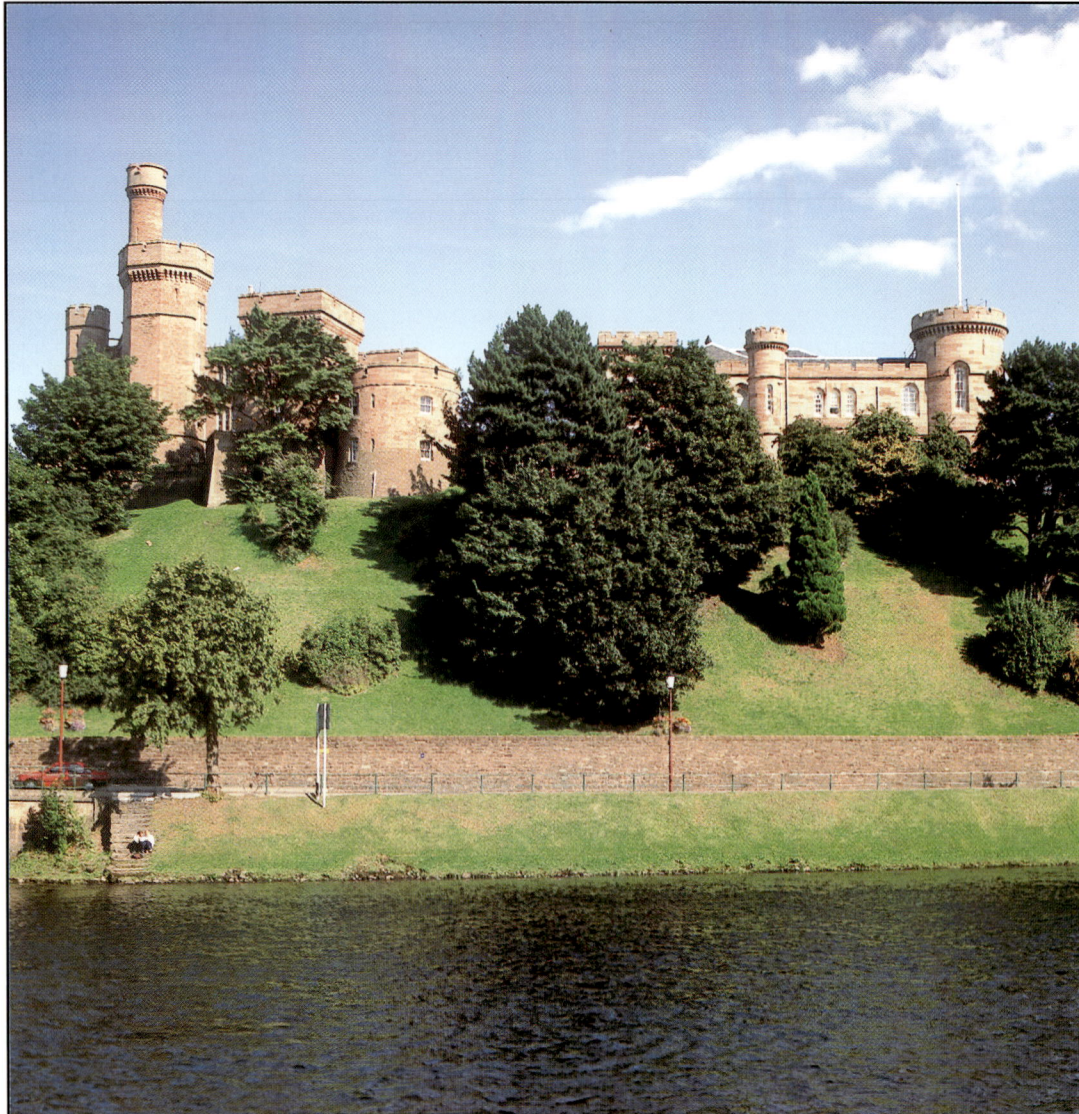

# *February*

19

23

20

24

21

25

22

*Notes*

26

2

27

3

28/29

4

1

*Notes*

## Tam o' Shanter
## A Tale
(Extract)

*Of Brownyis and Bogillis full
is this Buke.*
Gawin Douglas

When chapmen billies leave the
   street,
And drouthy neebors, neebors meet,
As market-days are wearing late,
An' folk begin to tak the gate;
While we sit bousing at the nappy,
And getting fou and unco happy,
We think na on the lang Scots
   miles,
The mosses, water, slaps, and
   styles,
That lie between us and our hame,
Whare sits our sulky, sullen dame,
Gathering her brows like gathering
   storm,
Nursing her wrath to keep it warm.

This truth fand honest Tam o'
   Shanter,
As he frae Ayr ae night did canter,
(Auld Ayr, wham ne'er a town
   surpasses
For honest men and bonie lasses.)

Robert Burns

*Auld Kirk,
Alloway,
South Ayrshire*

# *March*

5

6

7

8

9

10

11

*Notes*

# March

12

13

14

15

16

17

18

*Notes*

19

23

20

24

21

25

22

*Notes*

26

30

27

31

28

1

29

*Notes*

*April*

2

3

4

5

6

7

8

*Notes*

9

Dental Mr Ross 2-15.                13

10                                   14

11                                   15

12                               *Notes*

# *April*

16

17

18

19

20

*Dentist - Mr Ross 2 - 15*

21

22

*Notes*

# April

23

24

25

26

27

28

29

Notes

30

4

1

5

2

6

3

*Notes*

7

8

9

10

11

12

13

*Notes*

# *May*

14

15

16

17

18

19

20

*Notes*

# *May*

21

25

22

26

23

27

24

*Notes*

28

1

29

2

30

3

31

*Notes*

# *June*

4

5

6

7

8

9

10

*Notes*

**A Red, Red Rose**

Tune: Major Graham

O my luve's like a red, red rose
   That's newly sprung in June;
O my luve's like the melodie
   That's sweetly play'd in tune.

As fair art thou, my bonie lass,
   So deep in luve am I;
And I will luve thee still, my dear,
   Till a' the seas gang dry.

Till a' the seas gang dry, my dear,
   And the rocks melt wi' the sun:
O I will luve thee still, my dear,
   While the sands o' life shall run.

And fare-thee-weel, my only luve,
   And fare-thee-weel awhile!
And I will come again, my luve,
   Tho' 'twere ten thousand mile!

Robert Burns

# *June*

11

12

13

14

15

16

17

*Notes*

# *June*

18

22

19

23

20

24

21

*Notes*

25

29

26

30

27

1

28

*Notes*

2

6

3

7

4

8

5

*Notes*

9

13

10

14

11

15

12

*Notes*

16

20

17

21

18

22

19

*Notes*

*Inverness Castle,
by the River Ness,
Highland*

*July*

23

24

25

26

27

28

29

*Notes*

30

3

31

4

1

5

2

*Notes*

# *August*

6

7

8

9

10

11

12

*Notes*

13

17

14

18

15

19

16

*Notes*

*Brodie Castle, Moray*

20

24

21

25

22

26

23

*Notes*

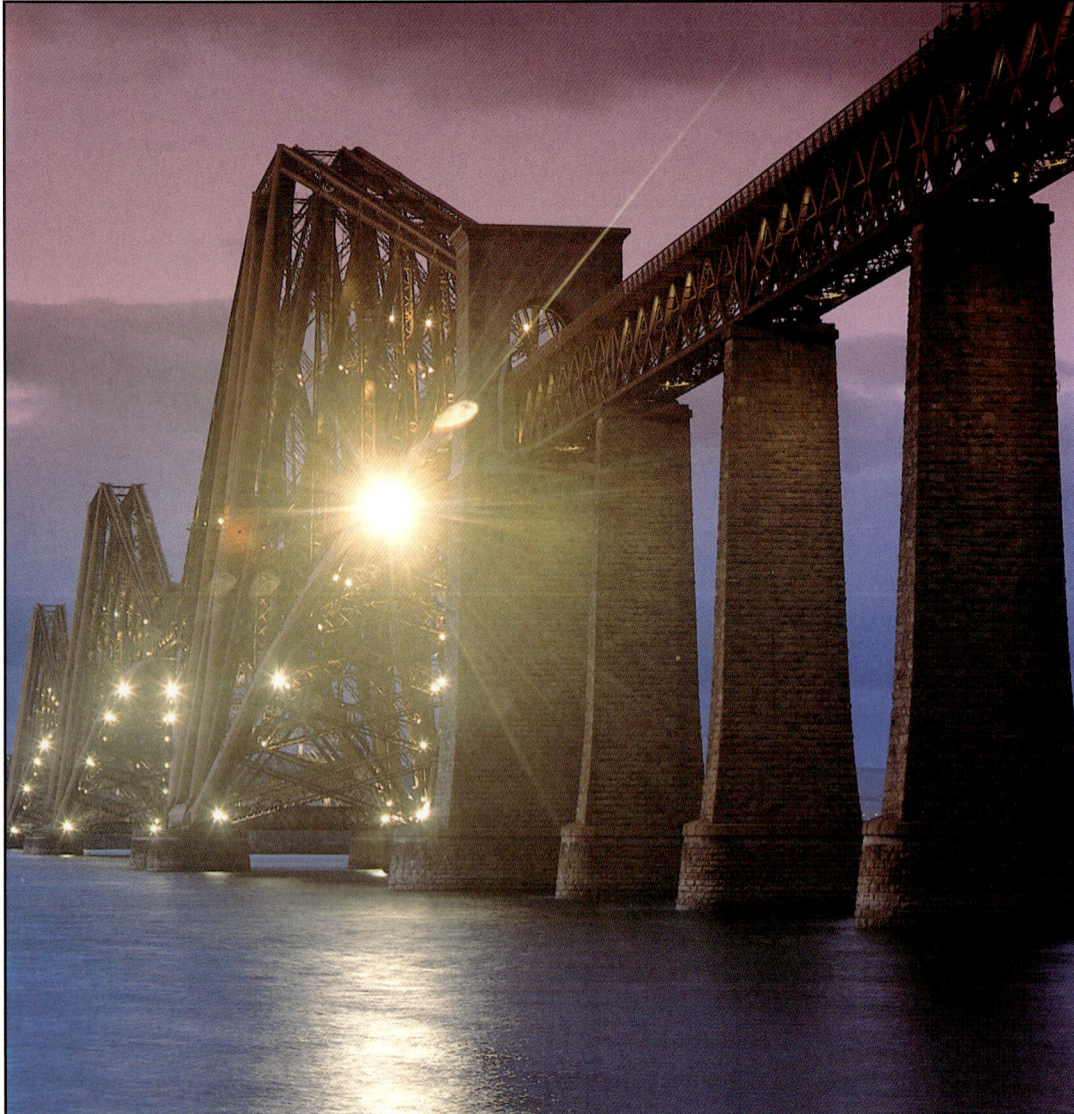

*The Forth Railway Bridge spanning the Firth of Forth and linking Edinburgh and Fife*

27

31

28

1

29

2

30

*Notes*

### Verses Written with a Pencil

over the chimney-piece, in the parlour of
the Inn at Kenmore, Taymouth (Extract)

Admiring Nature in her wildest grace,
These northern scenes with weary feet I trace;
O'er many a winding dale and painful steep,
Th' abodes of coveyed grouse and timid sheep,
My savage journey, curious, I pursue,
Till fam'd Breadalbaine opens to my view.
The meeting cliffs each deep-sunk glen divides,
The woods, wild-scattered, clothe their ample
   sides;

Th' outstretching lake, embosomed 'mong the
   hills,
The eye with wonder and amazement fills;
The Tay, meandering sweet in infant pride,
The palace, rising on his verdant side;
The lawns, wood-fringed in Nature's native taste;
The hillocks, dropt in Nature's careless haste;
The arches, striding o'er the new-born stream;
The village, glittering in the noontide beam—

Robert Burns

# September

3

4

5

6

7

8

9

*Notes*

10

14

11

15

12

16

13

*Notes*

*September*

17

18

19

20

21

22

23

*Notes*

September

24

28

25

29

26

30

27

*Notes*

# October

_____
1

_____
2

_____
3

_____
4

_____
5

_____
6

_____
7

_____
*Notes*

8

9

10

11

12

13

14

*Notes*

# *October*

15

19

16

20

17

21

18

*Notes*

22

23

24

25

26

27

28

*Notes*

29

2

30

3

31

4

1

*Notes*

# November

5

9

6

10

7

11

8

*Notes*

*Winter view looking southwest from the shore of Loch Laggan, near Inverness, Highland*

*November*

12

13

14

15

16

17

18

*Notes*

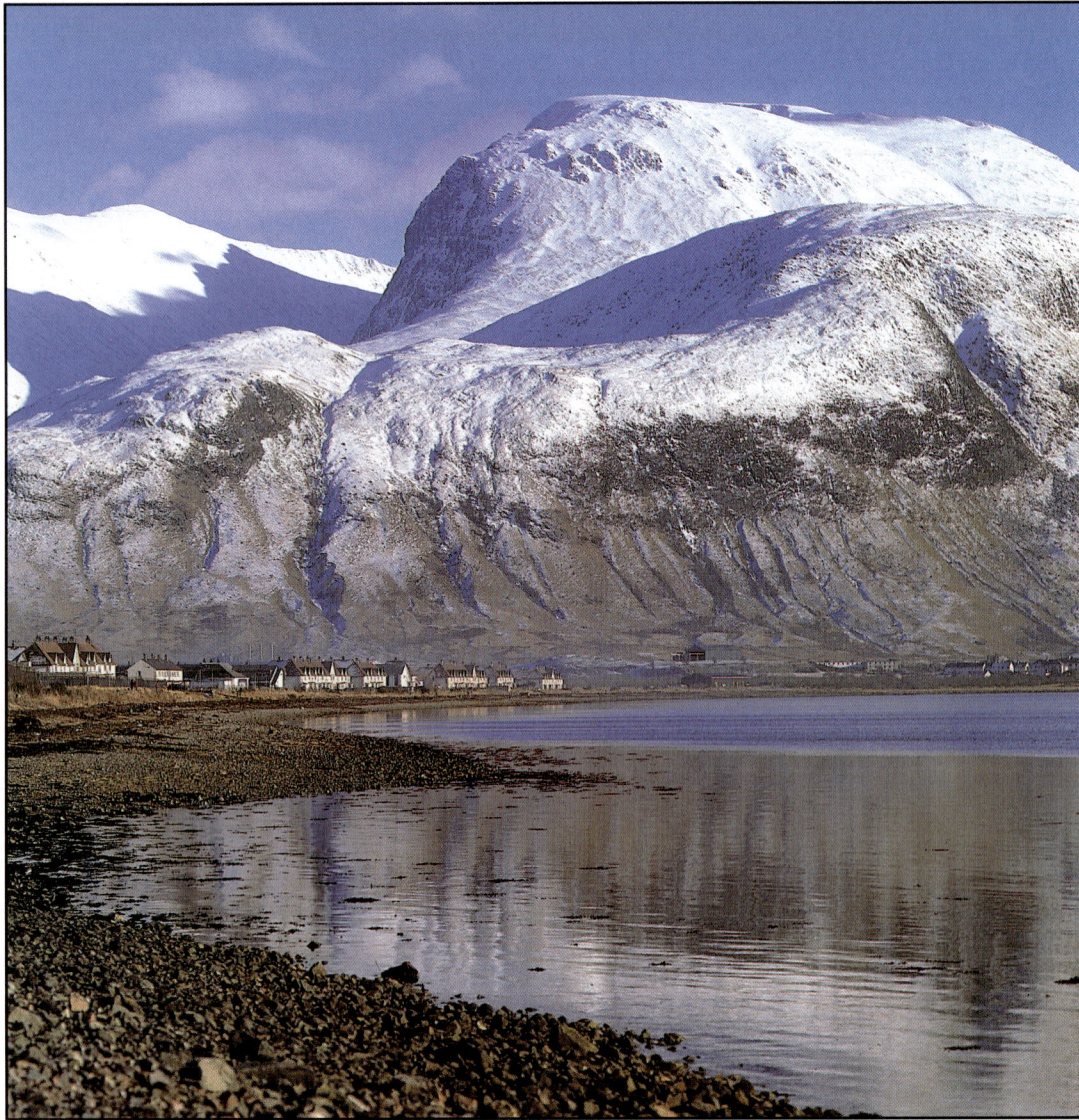

*Ben Nevis and Loch Eil from Corpach, Highland*

# November

19

20

21

22

23

24

25

*Notes*

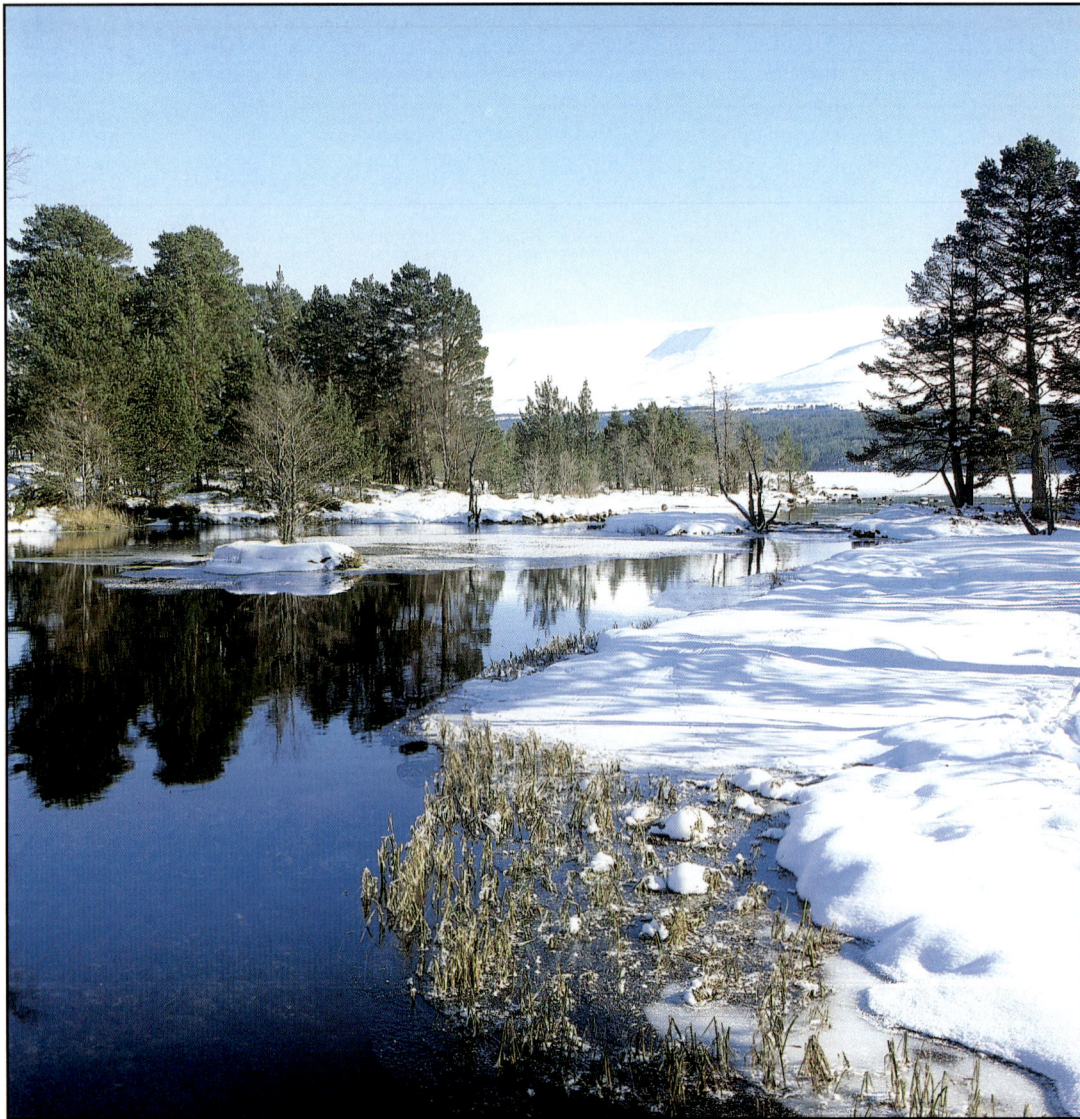

26

30

27

1

28

2

29

*Notes*

# December

3

4

5

6

7

8

9

Notes

# December

10

11

12

13

14

15

16

*Notes*

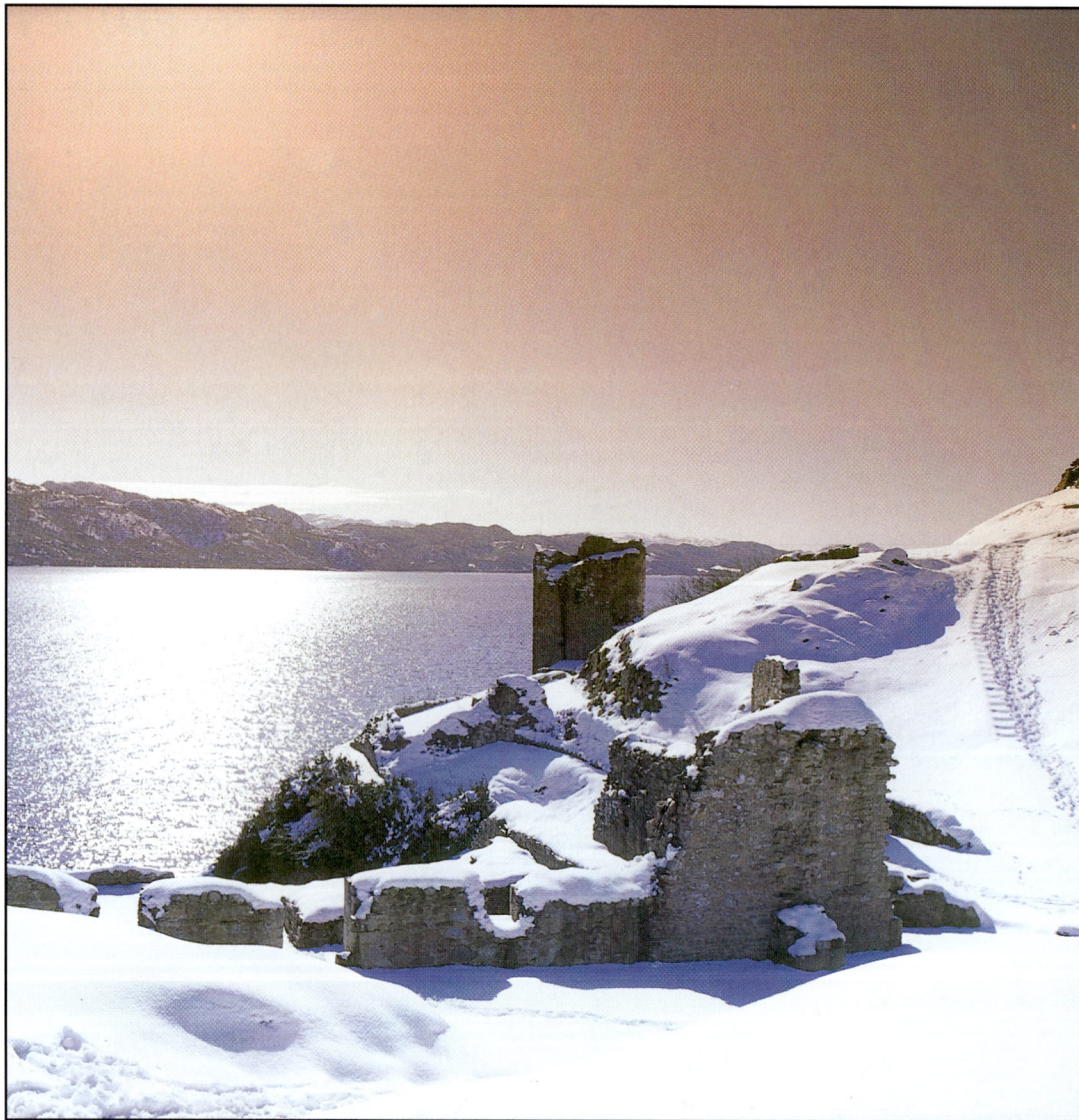

# December

17

18

19

20

21

22

23

*Notes*

## Auld Lang Syne

*For auld lang syne, my jo,*
*For auld lang syne,*
*We'll tak a cup o' kindness yet,*
*For auld lang syne.*

Should auld acquaintance be forgot
And never brought to mind?
Should auld acquaintance be forgot,
And auld lang syne?

And surely ye'll be your pint-stoup!
And surely I'll be mine;
And we'll tak a cup o' kindness yet,
For auld lang syne.

We twa hae run about the braes,
And pou'd the gowans fine;
But we've wander'd mony a weary fit,
Sin' auld lang syne.

We twa hae paidl'd in the burn,
Frae morning sun till dine;
But seas between us braid hae roar'd,
Sin' auld lang syne.

And there's a hand, my trusty fiere!
And gie's a hand o' thine!
And we'll tak a right gude-willie
   waught,
For auld lang syne.

Robert Burns

*Edinburgh Castle*
*Fireworks*

# December

24

25

26

27

28

29

30

31

# Addresses & Telephone Numbers

# *Addresses & Telephone Numbers*

# *Addresses & Telephone Numbers*

# Addresses & Telephone Numbers

# *Addresses & Telephone Numbers* *JKL*

# Addresses & Telephone Numbers

# *Addresses & Telephone Numbers*

# Addresses & Telephone Numbers

# Addresses & Telephone Numbers

# *Addresses & Telephone Numbers*

# *Addresses & Telephone Numbers*